# G[od]
# *the Father*

## REV. JUDE WINKLER, OFM Conv.

**Imprimi Potest: Mark Curesky, OFM Conv.**, Minister Provincial of St. Anthony of Padua Province (USA)
**Nihil Obstat: Francis J. McAree, S.T.D.**, Censor Librorum
**Imprimatur:** ✠ **Patrick J. Sheridan, D.D.**, Vicar General, Archdiocese of New York

The Nihil Obstat and Imprimatur are official declarations that a book or pamphlet is free of doctrinal or moral error. No implication is contained therein that those who have granted the Nihil Obstat and Imprimatur agree with the contents, opinions or statements expressed.

# THE HOLY TRINITY

BEFORE anything existed, before the world and all it contains were created, even before there was time, God already existed as God the Father, God the Son, and God the Holy Spirit. We call these three persons in one God the Holy Trinity.

The Father, Son, and Holy Spirit were so filled with love that they wanted to share their love with others. They decided that they would create the heavens and the earth and everything that is in them.

And so God the Father said, "Let there be light," and there was light. Every time that God spoke, He created something new. God created the heavens and the earth, the sun and the moon, the plants and the animals.

Everything that God created was good. God said that they were good and He blessed them. He ordered the animals to be fruitful and to multiply and to live all over the earth and in the sky and in the seas and lakes and rivers.

But God still wanted to create one more creature. God decided to create the first humans. He wanted the first man and woman to be very special and so God breathed His Spirit into them.

GOD truly loved the first man and woman. He named them Adam and Eve. God placed them in a garden and put them in charge of everything that they saw. They could eat the fruits and vegetables that they found there.

The only thing that God forbade them was to eat of the fruit of the tree of the knowledge of good and evil. God told them that they should never eat the fruit of that tree.

Instead of obeying God's command, Adam and Eve listened to the voice of the snake in the garden, the devil. The snake told Eve that God was jealous of them and wanted to keep the fruit of that tree for Himself.

Adam and Eve ate the forbidden fruit. As soon as they ate it, they realized they had done something very wrong. They hid from God because they were afraid God would punish them.

God called out for Adam and Eve and asked them what they had done. (God already knew, but He wanted Adam and Eve to admit their mistake.) God punished them for their sin, but He did not stop loving them. He continued to care for them even though they had sinned against Him.

# NOAH AND THE FLOOD

GOD continued to love Adam and Eve and their children and grandchildren. Yet, no matter how much He cared for them, they would always turn their backs on this love and commit greater and greater sins.

Finally, God realized that men and women had totally lost their way. They hurt everyone they could, and never obeyed God's commandments. They only cared about themselves.

God decided to send a great flood to punish people for their sins. But God still wanted to protect those people who were good and generous and obedient. He told Noah to build a great boat called an ark. Noah was to bring his family and all kinds of animals into the ark.

Noah did just as God had commanded him. When the boat was ready, God sent a terrible flood upon the earth. But Noah and his family and the animals in the ark were safe.

When the flood was over, Noah thanked God for all that He had done. God was very pleased with Noah so He promised him that He would never flood the whole world again. He also gave Noah a sign of His promise: the rainbow.

7

YET people continued to turn away from God's love and to sin. So God chose to reveal Himself to Abraham and Sarah and to ask them to leave their homeland and go to the land that He was promising them.

Abraham and Sarah left their families and traveled to the promised land. When they arrived, God made a promise to them that He would always be their God and they would always be His people. We call this type of promise a covenant.

God promised them that they would have many children and grandchildren—these would be more numerous than the stars of the sky and the sand on the shore of the sea. They would also inherit the land in which they were living.

One day God asked for a great act of trust on the part of Abraham. He tested him by asking Abraham to sacrifice his son Isaac. Abraham obeyed and was ready to sacrifice the boy when God sent an angel to stop him. He then knew that Abraham would always obey Him in all things.

For this reason, God blessed Abraham and Sarah. He made them the father and mother of His chosen people: the people of Israel.

# MOSES

THROUGHOUT their history, the people of Israel had many trials and difficulties, but God always protected and led them.

In the days of Joseph, He led them down to the land of Egypt so that they would not die of hunger during a terrible famine. Eventually the people of Egypt became jealous of God's people and enslaved them.

God then sent a great hero to rescue them, Moses. One day God appeared to Moses in the form of a burning bush. God told him that He was sending Moses to free the people of Israel from their slavery. Moses asked God what His name was so that he could tell his people who had sent him.

God said His name was Yahweh, a name that means, "I am." The people of Israel always believed that this was a very holy name, for God Himself had revealed it to Moses. They would not even read it aloud, for it was too sacred to pronounce.

Moses obeyed God's command and led his people out of Egypt into freedom. In the desert God appeared to him again and gave him and the people of Israel the Ten Commandments so that they would know how to please the Lord.

# KINGS AND PROPHETS

GOD guided His people under the leadership of Moses and Joshua and the Judges. Soon, though, the people of Israel told God that they wanted a king just like all the other nations of the earth. So God gave them kings who would govern them. He gave them Saul and David and Solomon and all of the other kings.

King Solomon built the temple to the Lord in Jerusalem. This was a place where God's people could worship Him in a special way. They realized that God was so great that He did not need a house in which He would live. Yet the temple was a place where God was always close to His people.

The kings were supposed to lead the people of Israel in God's ways, but they often led them into sinful practices. Instead of being faithful to God, they were often the ones who would worship false gods and teach God's people to do the same.

So God sent them Prophets, men and women who would speak in the Lord's name and call the people of Israel back to the truth. They would tell Israel how she was breaking God's law and tell her that God would punish her people if she did not change her ways.

# ELIJAH AND MOUNT CARMEL

ONE of God's great Prophets was Elijah. He lived at a time when the people of Israel were not always faithful to the Lord God.

One day Elijah challenged the pagan prophets and priests to a contest to see which god was the true God. They sacrificed animals upon an altar to their gods. The priests and Prophets of Israel then prayed to their God to send fire to consume their sacrifice, but nothing happened.

Elijah then prayed to Yahweh to send fire from the sky so that all would know that Yahweh was the only God. Fire immediately came from the sky and consumed the sacrifice. All the people then knew that Yahweh was the only God Who existed.

Another time Elijah climbed up Mount Sinai to meet the Lord. That is where Moses had met God in signs of fire and wind and earthquake. But this time God appeared to Elijah in a simple, gentle way. He did not appear in fire or wind or earthquake, but rather in a gentle breeze.

The meaning of this was that God does not always appear with great signs. Sometimes God reveals His love for us through everyday events and the people around us.

16

EVEN though the people of Israel had received proof that Yahweh was the only God Who existed, they continued to turn away from the true God to worship false pagan gods.

So the Lord handed the people over into the hands of their enemies. He allowed the armies of Babylon, a pagan nation, to conquer Israel and destroy Jerusalem. They burned everything in the city, even the temple of the Lord.

The people of Israel were frightened. They wondered whether God had rejected them forever.

So God sent Prophets to explain to his people that He still loved them. God had allowed Israel to be defeated as a punishment for their sins. But the time of punishment was now over. Sometimes we punish the people we love because we need to teach them an important lesson.

The Prophets revealed that God was a loving Father to Israel. He would never reject them for He loved them. God loved His people even more than a mother loves her children. God wanted to console His people. He promised them that He would restore them to their homeland. He would be their God and they would be His people.

# THE BIRTH OF JESUS

NO matter how many Prophets God sent to Israel, the people could not really understand Who God was and what God wanted.

Therefore God sent His own Son into the world. He sent an angel to Mary, a young woman who was engaged to Joseph the carpenter. The angel, Gabriel, greeted Mary with these words: "Hail Mary, full of grace, the Lord is with you."

The angel said that God had sent him to ask Mary to be the mother of the Son of God. Mary did not understand how this could happen, but she agreed to serve God with generosity. She said she was the servant of the Lord and that it should be done unto her as the Lord God willed.

Jesus was born in Bethlehem, born in a cave used to protect the animals living in the fields. Joseph protected Mary and the baby and served as foster father to the child.

When the child Jesus was twelve years old, He became lost in the temple in Jerusalem. Mary and Joseph finally found Him after three days and they asked Him why He had done this. Jesus reminded them that He had to be about His Father's business. Jesus was speaking of His Father in heaven.

## JESUS IS BAPTIZED

WHEN we say that Jesus, the Son of God, was born in Bethlehem, we are not saying that Jesus became the Son of God there. He was always the Son of God even before time began. But now God had entered into our world and had revealed to us Who and What God really was.

God continued to reveal Who He was and Who Jesus was throughout Jesus' life and ministry. When Jesus was about thirty years old, He went down to the Jordan River where John the Baptist was baptizing people. John wanted to be baptized by Jesus and not the other way around. But Jesus told him that this was the way it had to be, for this was His Father's will.

When John the Baptist poured water over Jesus' head, the heavens opened up and the Holy Spirit descended upon Jesus in the form of a dove. And the voice of God the Father said, "You are my Son, my beloved. In You I am well pleased."

The Father spoke from the heavens again when Jesus was transfigured on Mount Tabor. Jesus became as bright as a powerful light, and a voice from the heavens said, "This is My Son, My chosen, listen to Him."

# JESUS TEACHES US

JESUS was always teaching His disciples that God was both His own Father and their Father. He told them that God cared for us and loved us just like a loving parent.

This was not the normal way of speaking about God at that time. People spoke about God as if He were very far away. They believed that God did not have anything to do with our daily lives.

Jesus taught people that the exact opposite was true. God loved us so much that He had even counted the hairs of our head. Not one of those hairs would be lost without God knowing it.

He also taught His disciples that God was so loving that even the word "Father" did not quite reveal how much God loved us. Jesus taught His disciples that we should really call God, "Abba." This is a word from the language that Jesus spoke. It means "Daddy."

While Jesus was God the Father's Son because that is what He always was and always will be, we were being invited to become adopted children of God. In our Baptism, we became children of God the Father. God claimed us as His own and promised to protect us always.

# THE OUR FATHER

ONE day the disciples were listening to Jesus teach, and when He had finished they asked Him a favor. They had heard all sorts of prayers, and they wanted Jesus to teach them a special prayer that God would really like.

Jesus taught them that we should all call God our Father because He loves us as His very own children.

He then taught the disciples and us to pray to God, our Father, as follows:

OUR Father,
Who art in heaven,
hallowed be Thy Name.
Thy kingdom come,
Thy will be done on earth as it is in heaven.

Give us this day our daily bread,
and forgive us our trespasses
as we forgive those who trespass against us.

And lead us not into temptation,
but deliver us from evil.

## JESUS OBEYS THE FATHER

GOD the Father loved His Son, so He asked Him to be the most loving person that He could be. That is why the Father wanted Jesus to carry His Cross, and that is why Jesus was obedient to the will of the Father.

We had fallen deeper and deeper into sin and had no way of getting out of it. God loved us, but we did not believe it because sin had taught us not to love ourselves or anyone else. We were lost like the lost sheep of the Gospel.

God sought us out and told us that He forgave us and always loved us. Jesus told a story called the Prodigal Son about a son who sinned against his father, and yet the father forgave him. He not only forgave him, but even ordered a great celebration when the son returned home. That story was about how God would forgive us our sins if we would only reach out to Him

God the Father knew that we would not believe we were forgiven and loved unless He showed us how much that was true. So God called Jesus to the Cross. By the Cross, Jesus was telling us that He loved us so much that He was willing to die for us. The Father was very pleased with Jesus for being so generous in His love.

# THE RESURRECTION AND THE ASCENSION

GOD the Father called Jesus to the Cross, but He did not abandon Him. After Jesus was buried in the tomb for three days, God raised Him from the dead. This happened very early in the morning on the first Easter Sunday.

Jesus appeared to His disciples and continued to teach them for the next forty days. He explained why He had to die and rise to life. He had told them all of this before, but they had not been ready to understand what He was saying. Now that they had seen Jesus die on the Cross and rise from the dead, they were ready to listen and understand.

After teaching them for forty days, Jesus took His disciples out to a hillside outside of Jerusalem. He told them to preach to all the nations. They were to baptize them in the name of the Father, and the Son, and the Holy Spirit.

Jesus then ascended into heaven where He sits at the right hand of the Father.

God was so pleased with what Jesus did that He proclaimed Him to be Lord of the heavens and the earth and under the earth. This is why we bow our heads when we say the name "Jesus."

## THE HOLY SPIRIT

GOD the Father and Jesus also sent the Holy Spirit upon Mary and the disciples on Pentecost Sunday. The Holy Spirit taught the disciples about God and reminded them of what Jesus had told them and gave them the courage to preach God's word to everyone they met.

We also receive the Holy Spirit when we are baptized and again when we receive Confirmation. He lives in our hearts and teaches us and comforts us and leads us in God's ways.

Sometimes we are not sure that God hears our prayers because we do not receive what we are praying for. The Holy Spirit reminds us that God is our Father, our "Abba." This word means "Daddy" and tells us how much God loves and cares for us.

We do not have to be afraid of God. We should try to love Him and obey Him just as we love and obey our own father and mother.

Whenever we feel alone and afraid and confused, we should turn to our Father in heaven and pray the Our Father, the prayer that Jesus taught us. The Holy Spirit, Who lives in our hearts, will then remind us that God is our "Abba," our Daddy, and that God will always be there for us.

## THE SIGN OF THE CROSS

THERE are many ways to remind ourselves that God the Father loves us. One of the easiest ways is something that we do many times a day, making the sign of the cross.

Every time that we take our hand and touch our forehead, heart, and shoulders and we say, "In the name of the Father, and of the Son, and of the Holy Spirit," we remind ourselves of Who God is and who we are. Jesus, our Brother, and the Holy Spirit help us to pray and lift up our prayers to God, our Father, our Daddy.